LEAVING GIANT FOOTPRINTS . . .
WITHOUT STEPPING ON YOUR KIDS

Leaving GIANT FOOTPRINTS...
Without Stepping on Your Kids

Jim Wilcox

Beacon Hill Press of Kansas City
Kansas City, Missouri

Library of Congress Cataloging-in-Publication Data

Wilcox, Jim.
    Leaving giant footprints without stepping on your kids / Jim Wilcox.
      p. cm.
    ISBN 0-8341-1874-2
    1. Fatherhood—Religious aspects—Church of the Nazarene. I. Title.
BV4529.17.W55 2000
248.8'421—dc21

                    99-048415

10   9   8   7   6   5   4   3   2   1

To Dad, who made me a son,
And to Ben and Josh, who made me a dad,
And to the two women who helped in both.

Now

by Jim Wilcox

Then, I thought Dad was teaching me to ride a
    bike without training wheels;
      Now, I know he was showing me how to stand
        on my own two feet.
Then, I thought he was teaching me to construct
    a kite from newspaper and an old yardstick;
      Now, I realize he was encouraging me to fly.
Then, I thought he was forcing me to eat every-
    thing on my plate;
      Now, I realize he was teaching me the integri-
        ty of commitment.
Then, I thought he was teaching me to throw and
    catch a baseball;
      Now, I realize he was telling me that those
        who play together stay together.
Then, I thought he was helping me finish my
    math homework for tomorrow;
      Now, I realize he was showing me that learn-
        ing lasts a lifetime.
Then, I thought he was just reading me a bedtime
    story;
      Now, I realize he was teaching me that those
        who *can* and *have* must help those who
        can't and *have not*.

Then, I thought he was working for a living;
    Now, I know he was working for me.
And leaving giant footprints to follow.

1

THE DREADED DECLARATION OF INDEPENDENCE

"Then, I thought Dad was teaching me
to ride a bike without training wheels;
Now, I know he was showing me
how to stand on my own two feet."

IT ALL starts out so perfectly.

Bringing home your firstborn baby from the hospital is one of the most gratifying experiences for a new father. It's a day full of dreams and pride and . . . and . . . and . . . did I say dreams?

As you gaze into the face of your precious, slumbering infant, your heart swells with so much love, you think you just might explode. In your mind, you see her as the first woman president of the United States. Or you picture him as a Nobel prize winner for discovering a cure for the common cold. (I imagined my son as the future center fielder for the San Francisco Giants. Hey, you should have seen his hands.)

As the days become weeks, your child begins to look up at you as if you are the greatest human being who has ever lived. Talk about an ego trip.

9

That baby can make you feel like the strongest, smartest, fastest action hero in all Cartoondom. Forget Hercules. Forget Popeye. You're "The Great Daddini—Savior of Mankind!"

Eventually, those weeks become months. Your child's first step rivals Neil Armstrong's. Her first word is sheer poetry. And the day he actually puts a spoonful of baby oatmeal into his own mouth, you dash to the office with a video of the big event.

Finally, your infant-turned-baby becomes a child, and you are able to go outside and play with him. The worship grows even stronger when he sees you actually catch the ball. "How does Daddy do that?" he wonders to himself. "He must be the best athlete in the universe."

But that first time your child catches a pass or a toss, or a hand-off for that matter, you call your buddies and tell them the next Jerry Rice has been born.

"You shoulda seen it, Mack. He had his hands out like a real pro, Mack, a real pro! I laid the ball in there and he squeezed those magic hands together like he's been doing it all his life. Oh, Mack, it was the greatest thing I've ever seen. Ever!"

It is truly a Mutual Admiration Society. There's no doubt in your child's mind that if the world needed saving, if the Super Bowl was on the line, if the president needed to ask someone for crucial advice, you are the one to be summoned. "You Da Man!" And if you needed an assistant, "He Da Little Man!"

I hate to be the bearer of bad news, but that euphoria doesn't last forever, my friend. Somewhere around the age of 10 (curse those double digits) your No. 1 Fan starts to hang around other kids his age rather than you. He has made his choice—and it ain't you.

By the time he reaches high school age, Dad's stock falls off the chart. Instead of running fast, you run a little "funny." Instead of being the cleverest wit to utter the language, your jokes are really "dumb." Instead of driving like an Indy driver, you drive "so slow."

That sets up the moment of The Dreaded Declaration of Independence: the driver's permit. (You thought teaching her to ride a bike was tough. Wait for this training course. Oooohhhh boy!)

In most states, this phenomenon is legal at age 15½. In some, it's 14½. Others, at 15. If I were in charge of the world, a child would be able to climb behind the wheel of a 2,200-pound projectile and aim it down a paved path at 110 miles per hour at age Overmydeadbody!

Suddenly, you are no longer a "daddy." You may not even qualify to be a "dad." Nope. At this intersection of life, you find yourself hovering over the precipice that lies between being a used car salesman and a nark. You are the legal guardian, and might I stress the word, "legal," of a teenaged driver.

How did this happen?

One of the problems a father faces when this does indeed happen is captured in one word. Can you say "guilt"?

Suddenly all those stupid—and for many of us that starts with a capital S—things you used to do in, and on, and to a car come back to haunt you. That's exactly what scares you to death when this baby of yours insists on driving the family vehicle. You remember everything. March 20, 1996, is the day my memory went into overdrive.

The fastest I have ever driven a car was twice as fast as cars were meant to travel: 110 miles per hour. Now that sounds like "parking speed" to some of today's teenagers, but to me it was the speed of light. All completely legal, of course, because we were in Nevada (State Motto: We Park Cars Faster than That), where there are no posted speed limits—at least none that I could read at that speed.

Interestingly, the '64 Le Mans (French for "You Da Man") truly ran much more smoothly at 110 mph than it did at 55. Or 75. Perhaps because it was slightly airborne at that speed.

I actually learned to drive on a 1969 VW stick shift, which meant other drivers could *smell* me coming long before they could hear me coming, and they could hear me coming from up to five miles away.

My pattern of driving a stick shift back then—which would become my life's credo—was that once I got the thing into third gear, I would never leave it again. That meant, of course, that I often had to take corners at upwards of 35 mph just to keep the engine running. Why, once I drove from Portland, Oregon, to Nampa, Idaho, a distance of approximately 400 miles, in third gear. And there were very few corners on that trip.

I come from a long line of licensed loonies. Legend has it that my grandpa once hit a deer so hard with his '57 Bel Air that any time he turned on the defrost, he was treated to rather large chunks of venison jerky.

My mother insists on driving with her right foot on the accelerator and her left foot perched precariously on the brake pedal . . . "just in case." Traveling with Mom behind the wheel is like being on both the roller coaster and the bumper cars. A passenger's neck can literally be jerked completely off its rightful moorings.

During her driving test, my older sister was commanded to turn right off a busy, four-lane thoroughfare . . . which she did . . . obediently . . . from the *left*-hand lane!

I couldn't help but remember that, too, when my son flunked his driver's test for the second time when the instructor told him to turn right . . . which he did . . . obediently . . . onto a one-way street going *left*.

One of my most harrowing experiences in a car, however, came not with my son behind the wheel, but with Dusty driving.

Where and when I went to college, going to movies was somehow construed to breaking one of the Ten Commandments. Six of us defiant ones threw caution to the wind, anyway, and drove to a faraway drive-in theater to see "Lady Sings the Blues."

On our way back to campus, we noticed that a police cruiser had pulled up behind us and was tailing us pretty closely at 65 mph. A second glance—a second police car behind the first.

"Now why would two police cars be following us at midnight on the highway between Meridian and Nampa, Idaho? Uh?"

As we neared the turnoff, a third cop car fell

in line. We exited as lawfully and carefully as six boys in a '64 heap can exit and suddenly found ourselves not only with three cop cars behind us, but one in front of us. Like an escort. Straight to the dean's office. Then, as if that weren't enough, two more police cars came directly toward us. All for going to a movie?

At this point, all six cars turned on their spotlights, flashing red and blue lights, and sirens at the same time. It looked like World War II in downtown Berlin.

It was blinding.

It was deafening.

It locked my knees together.

In a split second, all 12 cops were out of their cars, ducking behind their car doors, brandishing 9 mm firearms, aimed directly at our GPAs.

Despite my brother's suggestion that we make a run for it, we were to find out that our vehicle fit the description of an armed robbery-stolen car incident in Meridian. We all had a good laugh when one of the cops recognized two of our friends as pals of his and we were "released." But my knees were still locked together the next day.

Almost as tightly as they locked the day my older son got in our Honda Accord with our younger son in the passenger's seat and drove for the first time alone down the street. Out of sight. Out of my control.

I should never have taken the training wheels off his bike.

2

THE SECRET LIFE
OF CREATIVITY

"Then, I thought he was teaching me to construct
a kite from newspaper and an old yardstick;
Now, I realize he was encouraging me to fly."

ONE UNIVERSAL TRUTH about dads is that
they all want a better life for their kids than they
had when they were young. (It's undoubtedly true
about moms, too, but they've already had their
day six weeks ago.)

This is perfectly illustrated in the tennis
shoes we wear.

I grew up with two pairs of shoes: one for
dress (which never wore out because we dressed
up only on Sundays) and one for everything else.
When our play got a bit more physical as we grew
older, we got a third pair so our school shoes
could be spared.

More than once I recall getting the old shoe
box lid out of the closet and cutting out a couple
of cardboard insoles so the holes I'd worn in the
soles of my tennis shoes would no longer leak and
soak my socks by first recess.

How fondly I recall the annual occasions of going to the local shoe store to get a new pair of tennis shoes. I can't tell you how excited I was. "Look at all the choices," I'd think. Black high-tops. Black low-tops. White high-tops. White low-tops. Wow!

With all the ceremony we could muster, my brother and I wiggled our big toes enthusiastically in pair after pair so my dad's thumb could tell if he was going to get his money's worth out of these new Keds or Chuck Taylor's. Wiggling patiently wasn't hard for John and me because we were basically wiggly by nature, and this was a particularly wiggly occasion.

Finally, when his approval met our joy, we'd box up the old shoes and wear the new ones out of the store, into the car, and all around the house. Even when bedtime came, it was hard to take them off—they smelled so good and felt so good and looked so good. Our dreams that night were filled with stretching singles into doubles, nay triples, breaking track records, leaping 10 feet into the air to snag a low-flying robin.

Things are different now, aren't they? Our children's choices are unlimited: dozens of brands, dozens of "models," hundreds of colors. Tennis shoes have become so sophisticated and complicated, they can be worn to just about any occasion one might be obligated to dress for. Even church on Sunday.

And since fathers never stop being children, really (the toys simply get bigger and more expensive), we, too, have several pairs of tennis shoes in our closet nowadays. Some are for yard work, some are for walking around the park, some are for our basketball leagues, some are for our work place, and some are just for wearing around the house during football season. We now buy tennis shoes more to relieve boredom with our old ones than to relieve holey insoles and wet socks.

And that may not be all bad, as I think about it, because boredom is the beginning of creativity. History records that Thomas Edison was bored one day—always nursing his bruises from running into furniture the night before—and created the modern-day light bulb.

Books also tell us that Alexander Graham Bell was tired of walking three miles to the pizza joint to get his dinner, so late one night, he invented the miracle of the telephone.

Few people realize that Benjamin Franklin was bored reading his almanac one summer day, so he went outside to fly a kite. Little did he know at the time that rain was in the forecast or that his keys to the liquor cabinet were stuck to the string. *Pop!* He discovered electricity (the hard way).

That's why I get a kick out of my own kids every Christmas vacation or summer break. Two or three days into it, they invariably come to the breakfast table or living room and announce to the world as if they are the only victims to have ever suffered——"I'm bored." That's the signal that things are really going to start happening around our place.

Out come the Legos and soon our house is filled with flying saucers that really fly. Or forts that can repel even the slyest of domestic cats. Or technical weaponry that shoots with deadly accuracy and lethal force.

Our older son has always been a frustrated "Fix-it" man. He may not be in the same league as *Home Improvement*'s Tim Taylor, but he's close. For instance, within hours after receiving a Fisher Price tape recorder for his sixth birthday, he had it taken all apart and spread all over the garage floor.

"Where does it store the voices, Daddy?" he wondered.

(That was the beginning of never being able to find all my tools.)

Even 13 years later, his car today looks nothing like it did the day he bought it. He has spent hours rewiring it so the alarms don't go off to warn him that he's not wearing his seatbelt.

"It's such an annoying noise, Dad," he whines.

I find it highly ironic, then, that he has also added about 16 speakers to the car's brand-new stereo system—which he installed by himself—so that his car can actually put cracks in the road's asphalt. I hope he becomes an electrician some-day and makes enough money to support me in my old age.

When our boys are bored now, they get out their guitars and write beautiful music. Granted, it's not all beautiful. Frankly, some of it isn't even "music." But while Ben has become quite a lyri-cist, Josh, the younger one, is turning out to be not a half-bad composer. (You think I could make any money off them?)

I still recall the Sunday afternoon when I was just a boy, and I found myself bored. I wanted to go outside to fly a kite. Since it was a Sunday, however, and we didn't go to stores on Sunday, we couldn't go down to the store to buy one. In-stead, my dad suggested we build one.

"Build a kite, Dad? You can do that?"

"Sure. Go get a section of yesterday's newspa-per and that old yardstick in the garage," he told me.

With a slice down the length of the yardstick, he was able to fashion the cross support. Carefully folding and unfolding the newspaper, he figured out how to make the necessary diamond shape. (I was watching genius and didn't even know it.)

A staple here, and a tied-off string there, and within minutes I had a kite with Saturday's sports headlines all over the front. It was the greatest kite I ever flew. Luckily for me, my family never owned a Franklin liquor cabinet. Or liquor, for that matter.

Years before Halloween became so controversial and dangerous, it was the apex of a child's creative year. Dressing up as someone else and canvassing the neighborhood for as much candy as a pillowcase or paper bag or plastic jack-o'-lantern could hold seemed like such an excellent idea.

I think I was a hobo pretty much every year. Not because there had been a blockbuster movie that summer about a hobo overcoming the forces of evil with little more than his trusty duffel bag. Nope—I was a hobo for one reason and one reason only.

The costume was available.

Every afternoon that preceded "the night of nights," I went out to the garage and found the necessary garments that would transform me into California's youngest, if not thinnest, hobo: my dad's lawn pants and frayed cotton plaid lawn shirt.

Because they were dirty and baggy and well-worn, they fit my perception of what it meant to be permanently on the road. After draping myself in Dad's dutiful duds, I dug into the barbecue stuff to fetch a brick of hobo disguise: charcoal. No hobo is complete without a five o'clock shadow.

A bandanna full of rolled up newspapers hanging from the shepherd's staff I had carried in last year's Christmas pageant topped it off. I had created an alternative persona that gave me the courage to meet strangers at their front door. I was ready for an evening of bell-ringing and sugar-scarfing that I would never forget.

In a way, it was this character-playing that gave me the daring and hankering to become a writer. It was the holey shoes that taught me, in their own strange way, how to fill gaps that lie between a writer and reader. It was Dad's clever newspaper kite that showed me how a word might be adapted artistically to fit a peculiar need.

It was creativity in our childhood home, and the creativity in my current home that have enabled my imagination to take flight.

3

THE INTEGRITY OF
COMMITMENT

*"Then, I thought he was forcing me
to eat everything on my plate;
Now, I realize he was teaching me
the integrity of commitment."*

THAT PARTICULAR California Sunday afternoon
was not unique. It was not even peculiar. In fact, I
think I can honestly say to you that it wasn't even
all that particular. "Sunny and warm" is what I remember about growing up in California. All the
time. Every day. "Sunny and warm."

(Except for that Sunday morning when I was
a kid and it snowed an inch in our neighborhood,
but as the Lord's *day of rest* would have it, the
snow was all gone by the time we got out of
church. Oh, and except for that Friday afternoon
when I had to dress up for some sadists' wedding
in 111-degree shade. Other than those two days
of 22 years of growing up in California—all the
time—every day—"sunny and warm.")

We had driven the 30 minutes on Highway 71
to Aunt Billie and Uncle Herb's house on Via Del

Robles (which I was quite certain was Spanish for "Here Lies Great Barbecue!"). But as fate would have it, Uncle Herb—a produce manager for a small local grocer, ironically enough—had forgotten to buy enough cobs of juicy yellow corn, and that meant an "emergency trip" to the market.

Now, you'll have to understand that this was back in the days when Christians did not go to supermarkets on Sunday. No. No. No. Christians named Wilcox did not even go to restaurants on Sunday. No. No. No. People worked in supermarkets and restaurants, and that meant that they were all violating commandment number four: Remember the Sabbath day, to keep it holy.

To buy something from a commandment-violator was tantamount to breaking the commandment yourself.

So my dad, a commandment-keeper from bow to stern, did what was purely instinctive for a man to do—he got in Uncle Herb's prehistoric Hunterwagon and went hunting for the mighty Corn on the Cob in Sabbath-violating country. (And just to make sure he wouldn't be spending eternity alone in hell, he took my twin brother and me along.)

Luckily, we got out of the store unscathed, a dozen fresh ears bagged, and back into the Hunterwagon for the short trip home. But I was just a kid and I couldn't wait. I hunkered down behind the front seats, down there where only feet are supposed to go, and dug my little paw into my left pants pocket.

There it was. Just where I had ingeniously slipped it moments earlier. Nobody had seen me then . . . and no one was going to see me now. I was safe.

My fresh, warm, salted-in-the-shell, four-lump peanut.

As quietly as my sinful hands could pinch, I squeezed the secret place on the peanut shell, the place that snaps open a peanut shell like an over-stuffed piece of Samsonite luggage, to get to those four morsels of sinfully delicious peanut.

Snap!

"What was that?" my dad charged, whirling around in his front seat like he had heard the beginning of World War III. "What was that snap I just heard?"

"Jim stole a peanut from the store," my brother calmly said. (He's gone on to become a saint.)

"Stole a peanut? From the store?" my dad glared. First at me; then through me. "Is that true, Jim? Did you steal a peanut from the store?"

I'm not sure what I was thinking at that very moment because I'm not even sure I was thinking at all: probably something like, "Well, that's what happens to little innocent children when they are taken to the store to break a commandment." But all I could say with my quivering lips was, "Yes."

"Herb, I think we'd better turn the car around."

"But I've got corn, Galen. I need to cook the corn," Uncle Herb said.

"But Jim took something from the store that doesn't belong to him. We need to go back," Dad said. "Don't worry, I'll explain everything to Billie, and I'll make sure to be standing in between you and her when I do it."

"Oh, OK."

And back to the store we went. With one hand quivering in my dad's giant man-hand and the other clutching a copper penny, I was ushered past the checkout stands, past the cashiers and people standing in their lines, past the carts and the magazines and the candy racks, to the back of the store. To the produce manager. Big and burly. And aproned.

"Go ahead, Jim. Do what you have to do," Dad said.

Head down. Hand out. "Here's a penny I owe you, sir," I whispered. "I took a peanut without paying for it. I'm sorry."

To this day, 40 years later, I have never stolen another thing.

Now, to be fair to my dad, he was probably every bit as nervous as I was, going back to that store and taking me with him to confess what seemed to me to be an absolutely heinous crime, confronting a stranger. But at the time, I figured he was in cahoots with the massive produce manager, and I was heading to my certain and swift execution.

That day was infinitely important to me—as a son, as a Christian, but most of all, as a future father. Dad taught me that asking God to forgive me of a sin was just the first step. Making restitution and confession—the brutally hard stuff—is an imperative second step.

He taught me that being a person of honesty and integrity, of commitment and follow-through, is not just what it takes to be a man, but what it takes to be a Christian man.

If you're a student with an assignment that you and your instructor have agreed upon, you do it because that's your end of the bargain.

If you're an employee with a task to do while you're at work, you do your best work because that's what a man of integrity does.

If you're a child with chores to do, you do them as well as you can, without being asked or told a second time.

If you're a parent with plans to see your

child's ballgame or recital or play, you allow nothing to break that commitment.

What he was really teaching me, however, probably without even realizing it, was that to be a Christian, I must treat every other person with whom I come into contact as if that person were Christ himself.

Would I steal a peanut from the Creator?

Would I do anything but my best for the Master?

Would I shirk my duty to Him? Would I accept mediocrity for Him?

No. No. No. And no.

A few years ago, I had a student in a freshman-level course brag in an essay that he had received $8.42 too much in change from a restaurant server. He wrote about showing it to his friends at the table and how they laughed at his "good" fortune. The poor young man even reasoned that this was God's blessing to a struggling college student who barely had two pennies to rub together most of the time.

I wrote in the margin of his paper, "$8.42 sure seems a cheap price for a person's integrity." I have no idea if that spoke to him or not. Frankly, I'm not even sure he read it. I hope he did. Or will, someday.

When our older son was about four years old,

my wife took him to the grocery store with her. I know I may be biased, but when Ben was little and dressed in his Osh Kosh B'Gosh overalls, he was about as angelic as a born-and-bred Okie could be. I loved taking him with me to the store because he got so much attention, and therefore, I got some too. (I'm a man starved for attention.)

When they got home, we were in the kitchen, unloading the treasures when Ben reached into his overalls' front pocket and exclaimed in four-year-old wonder, "Where did dis come fwom?" He was holding a little book of horoscopes that cover grocery store checkout counters.

I thought that was a good question. "Well, Benjamin, just where did that little book come from?"

His lip began to quiver. "I dunno. I must've took it accidenta-wee."

"Ben," I bolstered up the courage to say, "that's stealing." Déjà vu! "We're going to have to go right back to that store right now and return it to the manager."

To this day, Ben has not stolen again.
Thanks, Dad.
Thanks, Grandpa.

4

PLAYING TOGETHER—
STAYING TOGETHER

"Then, I thought he was teaching me
to throw and catch a baseball;
Now, I realize he was telling me that
those who play together stay together."

IT STRUCK ME like a physical force—almost
like a tangible entity. The aroma that wafted toward me somehow seemed to have the capability
of wafting me away from the heat and humidity
that surrounded me.

Where we live, we are not blessed with major
league sports, so we have reconciled ourselves to
being a minor league city with major league
dreams. Our brand-new minor league baseball
stadium is the centerpiece of a massive long-term
endeavor to revitalize the downtown area—kind of
like a San Antonio Riverwalk . . . Junior.

Even so, it still seems fun to go downtown oc-
casionally and watch a few innings of professional, albeit minor league, baseball. There's just
something about the beautifully coiffured grass,

33

overpriced concessions, and hard plastic seats that make us proud to be Mid-Americans.

But it's the smells of the ballpark that transport me to my youth. Having grown up in a Christian home, I was not often (as in nearly never) exposed to some of the more interesting fragrances known to humankind. My mother rarely wore perfume. My dad was allergic to aftershave. And even though we were of the hippie generation, my brother and I were never allowed to burn incense in the house.

But we all were sports fans, and we all worshiped the San Francisco Giants. Juan Marichal. Willie McCovey. Bobby Bonds. And my all-time idol of all sports—the "Say Hey Kid," Willie Mays. (I can still hear the public address announcer presenting the lineup: "Batting third, playing center field, number 24, Willie MAYS." I get goosebumps just writing it.)

Two or three times a season, we'd pack up the station wagon with as many blankets as we thought we could carry and make the 50-mile drive to Candlestick Park (home of the midsummer windchill index) to watch our beloved Giants play the hated Dodgers from Los Angeles—Don Drysdale, Sandy Koufax, Willie Davis, and Maury Wills.

As we entered the hallowed gates to find our seats, I invariably caught scent of what came to be known as "the smell of baseball." Undeniably forever linked to my youth . . . Beer and cigarettes.

Nowhere else would I ever have the opportunity to smell the mixed essence of "ice cold beer" and secondhand cigarette smoke. It meant I was at "the park," in the same arena as Willie Mays, vicariously hitting home runs and snagging impossible catches. It meant I could stay up late, whistle and scream as loud as I wanted, drop my peanut shells on the floor—on purpose. It meant family and home and playing together.

Today, I've carried on the Christian tradition of having a no-smoking, no-drinking household (I do allow my boys the occasional incense burn, however). And you know what? To this day, whether I'm at the Oklahoma City Ballpark to see the minor league Redhawks or back at Candlestick (3Com) on vacation to see Bobby's baby boy, Barry, belt a four-bagger, that unique bouquet of my younger days continues to mean one thing—I'm having the time of my life.

And no matter what number or name is out there in center field for the Redhawks, in my mind it's always number 24, and it's always Willie Mays.

My goal as a child was to one day replace Mays for the Giants. That's what made our neighborhood ballgames at Metzler Elementary School playground so absolutely important. They were training for the future as well as recreation for the afternoon.

Whether we had 18 guys show up, or 10, or just 3, the one who hit the longest home run and who caught the most exciting fly ball lived forever in the annals of time—at least until tomorrow's game.

Same time.

Same place.

Not anymore. Today, every child is signed up by his or her parents to play on organized, uni-formed, coached baseball teams. And basketball teams. And hockey teams. And soccer teams.

Seemingly gone from our streets are the neighborhood "pickup" games in the driveway or on the front lawn or in the street itself. Using ball gloves for bases. Taping a broken wooden bat for one more game. Appointing captains and choos-ing up sides.

My wife (who is both sport-illiterate *and* proud of it) and I decided early in our parenting to limit our sons' league sports to one per season— for the sake of our schedules, our sanity, and our marriage. We were not about to trade in our lives for a minivan and four or five games a night, no matter how much peer pressure they—or we— would face.

It's incredible how young this phenomenon begins. It seems that as soon as a child can walk, he or she is directed by some social force to don a uniform (usually red or purple), pick up the necessary equipment (at 10 times the cost we paid as children), and drag whichever parent is not in a coma on the couch to the kiddie-stadium to play. And to win.

Our introduction to this world of kiddie-competition was T-ball. The game that makes an hour seem like eternity. In fact, if a doctor ever tells me I have six months to live, you will find me at any T-ball game being played. It will make that six months seem like 60 years—or more.

Don't get me wrong. I loved watching our boys play baseball (and basketball and hockey and soccer), but somehow the game Abner Doubleday created in the mid-1800s is not the same game four- and five-year-olds play with a tee.

For one thing, they tend to run the bases backward—and that's if they hit the ball at all. Most of the time, they take three swings at the stationary ball, miss it three times and sit, disgruntled, in the dugout until their next at-bat.

When a ball is hit, however, all tranquillity is broken as the tyke runs clockwise (the natural direction, apparently) while everyone else on the field becomes a croquet hoop. First, the ball rolls through the "pitcher's" legs, then through the second baseman's legs, then the shortstop's, then the left fielder's and finally through the center fielder's legs. The ball eventually stops rolling simply from exhaustion.

The children seem to have a blast, especially after the game when candy and Coke are distributed, but I always had to be nudged awake. It seemed interminable.

Eventually, they graduated to "pitching machine" ball, which, for the first time, presents a moving target for them to focus their bats on. This, too, borders on being a spectator sport mostly because the pitching machine is vulnerable to nature's wrath and prone to grave inefficiency. *Bonk!*

Finally, they moved up to "real" baseball with a real human being on the mound, usually the only player on the opposing team with any eye-hand coordination at all. His primary purpose was twofold: (1) not to walk in 18 or 19 runs; and (2) not to kill anyone from the opposing team by beaning him in the eye.

This is where my sons lost interest in baseball. Winning became more important than playing (mostly to the coaches) and my boys rarely played, spending many an afternoon and evening on a hard wooden bench, tapping their empty gloves, and holding a cold aluminum bat in their hands.

But we still played the game together. Many hot summer afternoons or evenings, they'd call their friends and we'd all meet at the local schoolyard where I was named "Designated Pitcher." (I didn't mind. I had always fancied myself as a low-kicking Juan Marichal, anyway.)

I'd loft the ball plateward, they'd swing mightily, and we could almost hear the chants from the stands . . .

WILLIE!

WILLIE!

WILLIE!

There's no bigger thrill for a father than to play baseball with his sons. Even if you can't smell the aroma of beer mingling in the clouds of cigarette smoke, and they sometimes run the bases backward.

5

CURIOSITY KILLS ONLY CATS

"Then, I thought he was helping me
finish my math homework for tomorrow;
Now, I realize he was showing me
that learning lasts a lifetime."

MY FATHER was a genius.

I know most children think that when they're young, but I happen to be one of the few telling the truth (along with my own sons, of course).

He skipped a couple of grades early in his education, went off to college just days after he turned 16, was a member of a prestigious national scholastic organization, and, in the middle of his career, was accepted into an exclusive doctoral program at Stanford University in Palo Alto, California.

While attending college, Dad was also quite the athlete, lettering in baseball, tennis, track, and football. As quarterback, he once knocked over a receiver with a bullet pass. "Nice touch, Dad."

So I liked to boast in our childhood neighborhood bragfests that not only could "my dad beat up your dad," but he could out-negotiate him too. Ah, the power of the double-edged sword.

Dad found his professional niche not in the NFL (for obvious reasons) but in education, first as a teacher, then as an elementary school administrator. Mom, too, became an elementary school teacher after her nestlings began their own public schooling. Needless to say, our dinner conversations were basically, "So, what happened at school today?"

I don't need to tell you how awesome it was for an elementary school kid to have an elementary school principal for a father. Awesome . . . but sometimes awful. On the one hand, it seemed cool that my school principal knew my dad; on the other hand, it scared me that my school principal knew my dad. It certainly made my own behavior at school an imperative issue—both for Dad's and Mom's reputations and for my frail, little backside.

My twin brother, John, and I had quite a bit of fun looking alike. As geeky as we were, it was nice to have someone else who took some of the teasing once in awhile. Both rail thin, we were frequent targets of the more athletically-built kids at school. (I have since become more comfortable with my "body type," even presenting it to my college students as a "human missile.")

I stand straight in front of them, hands down to my sides, and say, "I was built for birth. Note the pointed, egg-shaped head—now balding—the narrow, sloping shoulders—the streamlined contours—the pogo-stick legs. I am quite certain that I barely fluttered the birth canal."

Truth be known, John and I, each around eight pounds at birth, did much more than merely flutter the birth canal. But hey, telling them that might ruin the story. My mom, who had to stay in bed the last six months of her pregnancy with us, sometimes wonders if we might have ruined her life. She still scowls when we enter the room.

At one point of my growth, I shot up to my present height of six feet-five inches, but was still hovering at 135-140 pounds. In fact, when I went to register for the Vietnam War draft, I was told I was too thin to fight. Something about being skinnier than the rifle I would have to carry. But that's another story.

One day at recess when we were in the sixth grade, my look-alike brother and I engaged in some apparently unacceptable behavior, whereby one of us would start up a meaningless conversation with a potential victim while the other one sneaked up from behind and got on all fours— right behind the victim's knees.

43

One little shove from the talking twin and *bam!* "Adios, amigos!" Oh, it was great fun.

Unfortunately, we were nabbed by some goody-goody and forced to write a 31-word sentence about the high cost of the criminal lifestyle 50 times. *"Fifty times? That's more than 1,500 words!"* we exclaimed. (We were both in the gifted math program.)

"Yep, 50 times. And it's due tomorrow."

Mr. Foglio, the teacher, might as well have condemned us to the gallows. We could never finish that huge of an assignment by tomorrow. Unless . . .

We hurried home before Mom or Dad could get there and ran to their bedroom, where in the top drawer of their bureau we knew they kept carbon paper.

"Yes," we shouted. "With this stuff, we can get the punishment finished in half the time." Then John reasoned, "If one sheet of carbon paper gets it done in half the time, two sheets would cut it to a third of the time." (He went on to become a math teacher, naturally.)

Now I'm not really sure why we returned the carbon paper to our parents' bureau drawer after we finished the 50 sentences, except that we must have thought that stealing was a far greater sin than deceiving.

Suffice it to say, Dad saw the used carbon paper in the drawer that evening, held it up to the light and read, "I have done a bad thing. In my selfish attempts to have fun on the playground, I have sent several of my classmates home with bruises. I apologize for my behavior."

His principal antennas shot toward the ceiling.

"Boys," he called. "Oh, boys!"

The punishment he dealt was much more painful than anything Mr. Foglio could have ever done. Legally.

Dad taught us a big lesson that night: tripping people violates a school rule but cheating violates a biblical rule. He also taught us that getting caught is immaterial to committing the wrong.

Dad taught us kids far more through example than he ever did through discipline, though. He taught us honesty and humility. When our home church suffered an awful rift due to some shady pastoral-board dealings, it was Dad, who had had no part in it at all, who stood in front of the entire congregation one Sunday morning and said, "I am sorry if I have offended or wronged any person in this fellowship. I've never meant to hurt anyone in my life." It was the first time I ever saw him cry.

Dad taught us that loving our mom was the

greatest gift he could give us. If ever a woman was treated like a queen, Mom wears a mighty large crown. From surprise gifts to unsolicited favors, from opening her car door to always serving her first, from listening to her every story to helping her daily around the house, my dad's sole purpose, it seems, is her happiness.

Dad taught us the value of an education. Going to night classes after work, he earned a teaching certificate so he could leave carpentry for teaching, and then a master's degree so he could leave teaching for administrating.

He taught us that learning math and English and science and history is important. Not only did we see him doing our taxes, writing Sunday School lessons, figuring angles in home repairs, quoting those who lived decades ago, but he was able to sit down with his kids and help them with their algebra and geometry when it made absolutely no sense.

But the greatest lesson he taught us was that we were valuable to him. In the middle of his doctoral studies at Stanford, a program he both loved and excelled in, a degree that would have enabled him to become an administrator on the district level or beyond, he pulled us all to the kitchen table one night and said, "In talking to your mother, I have decided that you need your dad more than I need an advanced degree. You are entering your teens, and believe it or not, you're gonna need me around more than I could be if I continued at Stanford. I just wanted you to know that." And he was finished.

But learning is never finished. To this day, I remember his commitment to his kids—in spite of his own ambitions, in spite of professional pressures, in spite of personal prestige—more than anything else he taught us. And because of his example, the thing I am proudest of today is that my own two boys know their father . . . and love him anyway.

Soon after Mom and Dad retired from teaching, they realized they weren't finished. Not really. So for little pay but huge rewards, they volunteered three years of their lives to teaching conversational English in Japan. It's safe to say, these were the three most gratifying and satisfying years of their careers.

Nearing 80 now, my father still teaches conversational English to Asian immigrants in his community—as well as a weekly Sunday School class at church.

Learning lasts a lifetime.

I, too, have become a teacher—as did my sister and my brother. We are all voracious readers. My brother and I do as much writing in our jobs as we do anything else. We both thrive on solving problems, building pieces of furniture, studying the great minds of the past. Our curiosity never seems satiated.

That's just the way we grew up.

6

A Cup in His Name

"Then, I thought he was just
reading me a bedtime story;
Now, I realize he was teaching me
that those who can and have must
help those who can't and have not."

ONE OF THE BEST THINGS I learned while growing up is that a person is inevitably measured by how much he or she leaves behind after he or she is gone. This was illustrated profoundly when Paige entered our lives.

A new member of my parents' Sunday School class, her life was in trauma. Her new husband was in a coma at a local hospital and Paige had no idea what would happen if he didn't make it. Weeks dragged into months, and finally, Richard died, leaving her a young and lonely widow.

For two years, Paige became a second sister to John and me. She ate with us, went to church with us, and practically lived with us as the Lord helped her get her life back together. For two years, my family lived out Gal. 6:10—"As we have opportunity, let us do good to all people, especial-

ly to those who belong to the family of believers"
(NIV). And the love my parents showed Paige came
back from her to us a hundredfold.

One of the primary reasons any person
strives to become a teacher is to "pass it on." The
allure of instructing is certainly not in the salary
or the hours or the prestige. The greatest joy in
teaching is giving back all that you've been given.
Years ago, at the beginning of my career, I learned
this truth in a powerful way.

I was so proud when I was hired to teach
writing at Southern Nazarene University in
Bethany, Oklahoma. Only 26, I felt about the
same age as my students, which made it both exciting and nerve-racking. But mostly I felt proud.
Too proud.

Seemingly every morning, strolling across the
mall with a burlap sack in one hand and a poker
stick in the other, corduroy jacket and an "old
man's hat" pulled low, was a man obviously in the
twilight of his life. I could see him from my third
floor office. "Was he a maintenance man who had
been absent the day the uniforms had been is-
sued?" "Was he a local loon, lost on his way
home, looking for something to keep or eat?"
"Should I report him?"

After several weeks, I grabbed another
teacher who had been at the school for several

years and asked her about this "weird guy with the gunny sack."

"Oh, that's Dr. Floyd," she told me. "He used to teach here. About 40 years, I think. History."

"Is that the same Fred Floyd whose name is on the Fred Floyd Center at the church across the street? That Fred Floyd?"

"The very one," she said, smiling.

"What in the world is he doing down there with the stick, the sack, the hat?" I asked.

"Picking up trash, it looks like," she said.

"Why?"

"Oh, he probably wouldn't want you to find out, but you'd have to really know Dr. Floyd to understand why."

Now I was really curious.

"He picks up students' trash," she continued, "because he loves students. And he loves this college. It's his way of remaining a part of students' lives. To pick up their trash for them. 'They're in such a hurry,' he would probably say, 'but I'm not,'" she said.

To Fred Floyd, being a college professor meant being a servant.

To my father, being a Sunday School teacher meant being a servant.

The other night, Josh got home 45 minutes after his curfew, and so there I sat in the living room to greet him. My speech was well-rehearsed; after all, I had delivered it dozens of times to his older brother over the years. As I began, I asked him why he was late.

"We were all praying at the lake, and a couple of women who were drinking and smoking asked us what we were doing. So we told them, and I was sharing my testimony with them . . ."

I interrupted. "You're late because you were witnessing to two women, sharing with them the love of Jesus?" I asked. I was having a hard time holding back my tears.

"Yes, Dad," Josh said.

My hard heart melted and my practiced speech disappeared. "Go to bed, Josh. I'm so proud of you."

All was right with the world.

7

A LETTER TO MY SONS

"Then, I thought he was working for a living;
Now, I know he was working for me.
And leaving giant footprints to follow."

I COME DANGEROUSLY CLOSE to plagiarism with this one, but as William Faulkner once said, "Everything goes by the board: honor, pride, decency . . . to get the book written. If a writer has to rob his mother, he will not hesitate."

Years ago, I was introduced to a short book by Marian Wright Edelman, a longtime child advocate and Washington change-agent, titled "The Measure of Our Success," and subtitled "A Letter to My Children and Yours." Her third chapter is called "A Letter to My Sons," and her fourth, "Twenty-Five Lessons for Life." They really dovetail nicely into one another.

That's why I'm combining those two ideas into this personal letter to my boys (even though I'm letting you read it too). The fact of the matter is, I think I'm writing it more for myself, looking at and back, than I am for them looking forward—always looking forward.

See if it hits you anywhere close to where you work and live and have your being these days. If it does, let out a giant "Hooo-aahh." If it doesn't, grab the remote—you've got better things to do.

Dear Ben and Josh:

As you now near that threshold to the Next World, the world of car insurance, and 1040 Schedules A and B, and monthly bills, and mortgages and marriage and kids of your own, I think it's time we finally had that father-son talk you've so looked forward to.

Don't worry—it's not about *sex*. You probably already know more about that than I do, anyway. (Though I must know enough to have gotten it right at least twice in my lifetime.)

Some of these "survival tips" I've learned through just being your dad. Others I've learned from being your mom's husband, and some I've learned from being your grandparents' son. Some I picked up from my employers, some from my students, some from the people I work with. And a few I've learned simply by watching other people when they weren't particularly looking.

These are the legacy I leave you.

I

Take neither yourself, your successes,
nor your failures too seriously.

The people who spend half their incomes on counseling and therapy, and most of their sleepless nights twisted in fret and worry, are the sorry souls who look in the mirror each morning and see someone who makes the world rotate evenly on its axis.

Nobody is that important—not even the guy you see every morning in his new black Mercedes, gabbing on his cell phone, heading for his private jet. He just thinks he is.

People who indulge themselves in self-congratulation or self-flagellation end up alone and very, very lonely.

To remain spiritually balanced and psychologically healthy, it is best to deflect the praise and reflect on blame. Earn your success and learn from failure. Never, ever, be afraid to fail.

And that brings me to my next point.

II

Failure is the salt that flavors success.

I earned straight A's only one quarter of college. Never in high school. Never in graduate school. Just one quarter of my junior year at Northwest Nazarene College (whose motto is We Give A's by the Bushel!) in little Nampa, Idaho (whose motto is This Spud's for You!).

Lucky for me, just the quarter before, I had

earned my first and only F in a course called "Constitutional Law." There I was, a wandering literature hack, stuck in a roomful of future litigaters and litigants, studying cases and precedents and torts I could barely pronounce, much less memorize, being drilled by a man in a pinstriped shirt who walked with a menacing limp that made my hair stand on end.

Bbbbbbbrrrrrrrrrr!

Do you think I would have felt one-tenth the thrill of those four A's in the winter term if I hadn't cried through the last half of fall quarter?

Noted author Anthony Campolo asked 50 men in their 90s to tell him what they would do differently in their lives. One universal answer was, "I would risk more." They had learned the value of failure.

III

Intelligence is measured less by the ability to answer questions than it is by the agility to ask them.

Anyone with half a brain can figure out the answer to a math problem or the correct response to a client's inquiry or a customer's request. Anyone!

But the impressive minds who have impacted the world with their passion and fervor are the "curious Georges" who have lived before us and among us—asking questions.

That's why journalists—the true ones—are among the world's finest minds.

That's why researchers give the world historical direction.

That's why explorers of all fields are the giants of progress and pain.

Jesus, himself, said in Matt. 7:7, "Ask, and you will be given what you ask for. Seek, and you will find. Knock, and the door will be opened" (TLB). He knew the value of the genuine inquiry.

IV

*Don't believe everything you read or hear—
but with all your heart believe everything
you write or say.*

If you believed the media, you'd be dead because no one can *look* like that, *eat* like that, *smell* like that, *sound* like that, *drink* that much beer—light or otherwise, *consume* that much cola —jolted or caffeine-free, *earn* that much money, *drive* that much car, *chase* that much American Dream, and survive. To borrow a line from the late Perry Como, "It's impossible."

That is not to say that we must all grow up to be cynics and fatalists, nosireebob! But a healthy dose of skepticism when it comes to the messages of this world never hurt anyone.

When it comes to the things we say or write down in life, on the other hand, well, the psalmist held no punches: "Let the words of my mouth and the meditation of my heart be acceptable to you, O LORD, my rock and my redeemer" (19:14, NRSV).

If you want to become men of integrity, have conviction about the words of your mouth and the meditation of your heart.

V

Look at the BIG PICTURE—
Use a telescope instead of a microscope.

I have wasted way too much of my life analyzing minutia, focusing so hard on the moment that I forgot to seize the day.

Your mom has a way of weeding through the immediate in order to find the imperative: "If it's not killing small children in a third world country, then it's not really *that* important."

When confronted with decisions and dilemmas and distractions, boys, ask yourselves these three questions:

If this were my last day on earth, would I do what I'm considering?

Will any of this really matter in 30 years? Or 30 days? Or 30 minutes?

Is this really how I want to be remembered?

VI

*Eat at least one meal a day with
the whole family at the table with the TV off.*

It hasn't been that long ago—why, when I was
a little kid, as a matter of fact—that television did
not rule the world.

Parents were not obligated by some unspoken
cultural decree to sign their kids up for T-ball,
baseball, hockey, two basketball teams, and 17
soccer leagues. Children did not have three part-
time jobs after school to pay for the hottest rod in
the neighborhood. Families did not bring home
dinner in a bag or pull breakfast out of the freez-
er.

Life is so much more complicated now—despite what we're told by manufacturers. But is it
really that much better?

VII

*Say "please" and "thank you" and
"excuse me"—especially at home.*

Why is it that often we are kindest to
strangers?

At the restaurant: "May I please have a ham-
burger, french fries, and a shake? Thanks." At the
mall, "Excuse me, but would you tell me where I
can find the sales rack? Thank you so much."

Then we sit down with the *people we love* and

say things like, "Give me that meat, will ya?" Or, "Get your feet off the couch, Pigpen!"

I'm not sure I've ever understood that. If I love you the most, shouldn't I treat you the best?

VIII
Love your job.

Can you imagine spending 40 years of your life, working only for a paycheck? What a wasted life!

When I was pondering my own future after college, a friend of mine gave me some great advice. He told me to write down the three careers I would love the most. I wrote:

Rock and roll singer

Editor of a small-town weekly newspaper

Professional comedian

Then I went to graduate school and became a college professor. But you know what? Twice a year our campus has a variety show, and several times I have rocked and I have rolled with the best of them.

Part of my role on campus is to be the adviser of our campus weekly newspaper, where I write a column and help produce a paper. And three or four times a day, I have a captive audience for my off-centered sense of humor.

I love my job!

IX

Remember every anniversary.

My dad has been married to my mom for well
over 55 years, yet to this day, he gives her a gift
and/or a card on the anniversary of their first date.

So I had the advantage of growing up, thinking this romantic memory was normal behavior
for a husband. Unfortunately, God has given me
an obsession for dates, so I can recall not only the
anniversary of the first date (October 29), but also
the first time we held hands (December 15), the
first kiss (January 7), the first "I love you" (January 19), the night she proposed (April 4), the night
I gave her the ring (July 5), as well as the wedding
anniversary (November 26).

Now if I could just remember where I put my
car keys.

X

Don't forget you have a last name.

This is the signal of maturity.

If immaturity is pleasing, thinking about,
seeking for yourself, then infants have got to be
the most selfish of all human beings. No matter
what time it is or what anyone else in the world is
doing, they expect the rest of humanity to stop
until their own personal need is met. And they'll
scream until it is.

But when a boy realizes that he is not only an individual but also a reflection of the generations that have created him, and of the generations that will follow him, then he has become a man.